T0194627

Preparation

BEFORE

Presentation

Be Still,
Be Expectant,
Be Victorious

CHRISTINE M. VILLASENOR

WESTBOW
PRESS®
A DIVISION OF THOMAS NELSON
& ZONDERVAN

WestBow Press books may be ordered through booksellers or by contacting:

WestBow Press
A Division of Thomas Nelson & Zondervan
1663 Liberty Drive
Bloomington, IN 47403
www.westbowpress.com
1 (866) 928-1240

Scripture taken from the King James Version of the Bible.

ISBN: 978-1-9736-6146-7 (sc)
ISBN: 978-1-9736-6145-0 (e)

Print information available on the last page.

WestBow Press rev. date: 5/16/2019

Contents

Introduction

If you feel in your heart that God is calling you to ministry and you don't know where to start or what to do with what is going on inside of you, chances are you are on the right track. This book is about being prepared to begin to fulfill the calling of God in your life. Your first and foremost calling is drawing near to God Himself so that He can use you.

Maybe you hear God's voice calling and pushing you. It is because you and only you are called to fill in the gaps of service where and when God needs you. The question is: Where do you think God is leading you? When you hear people say, "the calling," it could mean anything that surrounds you—ministering to your neighbor, coworker, community, or foreign missions.

So many times people start to take action to move forward but never finish the course or the task. These require baby steps and take time. Once you sense that God is calling you to speak to your neighbor or go to the mission field, you will never be satisfied with anything else until you take that first step in faith. I have been there several times, feeling defeated, frustrated, and suffering. The tugging in your innermost being will never be peaceful and at rest with God or in the things of God until you mean business and step out. Once you step out, God will step up.

When you feel frustrated or defeated, there will always be questioning, pondering, doubting, and asking, "Me, God? Is this really Your voice I am hearing?" I like visualizing that old war propaganda poster of Uncle Sam, with the big white glove pointing straight ahead and saying, "I want you!"

The calling or task that God has for you to do is never finished, so we often have the tendency to think, *If I finish that class that I have been teaching for twenty-five years*, or, *If I step out of a certain ministry and just take a rest*, or whatever excuse may be in your mind, then we have completed something. We think that now we can stop, and God understands. However, if you are truly honest with yourself, you will find that the call of God never stops; it continues until Jesus comes.

My favorite scripture that has kept me going is 2 Peter 1:10: "Wherefore the rather, brethren, give all diligence to make your calling and election sure: for if ye do these things, ye shall never fail." We have a responsibility to make our calling and election sure to fulfill scripture. Maybe you wonder, *How do I do that?* Well, you do that by first acknowledging the calling or the passion of serving God, then pursuing it through prayer, the Word of God, and counsel. Always pursue your call by these three.

His Word is truth and life. It will never lead you astray. First Corinthians 1:25–27 says:

> *Because the foolishness of God is wiser than men, and the weakness of God is stronger than men. For ye see your calling brethren, how many wise men after the flesh, not many*

mighty, not many noble, are called: but God hath chosen the foolish things of the world to confound the wise, and God hath chosen the weak things of the world to confound the things which are mighty.

I would rather be used by God as foolish and weak because then and only then will I rely on God and only God. That is exactly what He is after. I trust, rely, and depend on You and only You God.

I truly pray that you enjoy this adventure. But most of all, I pray that your adventure begins as a result of encouragement found in these pages.

Some other scriptures for you to look up regarding the calling of God include:

Ephesians 4:1–6
Philippians 3:14
1 Thessalonians 2:12
2 Thessalonians 2:14

Chapter 1
PREPARATION

Acknowledge the call of God in your life.
—Philippians 3:14

I press toward the mark for the prize of the high calling of God in Christ Jesus. Time goes by so fast, but I am learning that this too is part of the preparation process; "slow" is the word. Frustratingly slow. The past months have been trying and so busy working, and working, such is life right!

What is preparation? It is a time of study and prayer, recognizing and acknowledging the divine calling of God in your life, learning to be spiritually minded, having confidence, and knowing when to go or act. As I mentioned in the "Introduction," 2 Peter 1:1–10 speaks about our divine nature as a Christian and making our calling and election sure. Verse 1 says, "His divine power has given us everything we need for life and godliness through our knowledge of him who called us by his own glory and goodness." We are spiritually set through Jesus our Lord; our part is to take the first step out of the box, by faith; He will keep us as we do.

Working with the Holy Spirit is key to moving out into the fields of God's harvest. As we allow the Holy Spirit to do

His job in our lives, will we begin to recognize that we are on the right path. This takes time and is vital because as human beings, we have the awful tendency to think we know the best direction for our lives, and with this thinking, we could wind up on the wrong path which could result in frustration experiencing problems or stumbling blocks.

As I mentioned in the first paragraph of this chapter, life gets in the way, and the process of preparation becomes slow. Time, study, prayer, and seeking His guidance through His Word are all essential for our growth. How many times have I wished to just jump on a plane and go? I was thinking that God would just rush us out in to any mission field. I am so thankful for the times God has said, "No," or, "Not yet." I am sure He saved us from so many mistakes.

The Word of God says for us to study to show ourselves approved unto God: "A workman that needeth not to be to be ashamed, rightly dividing the word of truth" (2 Timothy 2:15). I want to encourage you to covet those times of quiet preparation, when you are in prayer seeking His will and obtaining divine direction. As you begin to sense Him leading, you will discover more and more new insights through His Word, leading and guiding you.

It was only a few years ago that my husband came to me and said he felt God was going to send us to Israel after three or four years of seeking and asking the Lord where He would send us. So as we will be teaching and bringing the Word of God to Israel, we must begin to make the necessary preparations for the land and for ministry. We need to study the history and culture of the people of Israel so that we will be confident there, living among the people when the time comes.

Israel is one of the most difficult places to minister. Having friends who live there, who have shared with us stories of daily living, the culture, and nature of the people (or as one of our dear friends puts it, "The people are a prickly pear," prickly on the outside, but sweet on the inside once they are opened up). It is a difficult field but God's Holy Spirit is there amidst His beloved Israel. No matter where God sends you, it is important to be filled with His love for the people.

So how does this begin to happen? It begins with a stirring in your inner person, or as the King James version says, "your innermost being." Another of my favorite scriptures is 2 Timothy 1:6–7: "Wherefore I put thee in remembrance that thou stir up the gift of God, which is in thee by the putting on of my hands. For God hath not given us the spirit of fear; but of power and of love, and, of a sound mind."

There is so much to say about these scriptures. I don't know about you, but I want to constantly have the gifts of God stirred up inside me. I want to be able to act and move forward with God without fear. Whenever I have felt prompted to do something in service to the Lord, I have learned to put it on the shelf in prayer. I have noticed that if it is of God, it will come back into my heart over and over. Other times, it is so clear that there is no question.

About five months before my first mission trip to Russia, we began to seek the Lord, asking, "God, what is it you want us to do? Where do you want us? Where do you need us?" If you are praying this way now, look out because God will answer you. One Sunday we were sitting in church, and they announced that our senior pastor had just come back from Russia, where the church supports orphans at four orphanages. Well, months before, Raul and I also had a suspicion that God was calling us to missions, but we didn't know how or where; nor was it confirmed. I was thinking, *Okay, I am really off my rocker. There's no way I am going to be a missionary!*

That Sunday, when our pastor came out and began to share, we both broke down and wept. Our pastor was not sharing something emotional or sad about the children; it was purely the power of the Holy Spirit that fell upon us. Without saying a word to each other, we knew we had to go. Why? I honestly think that it was strictly because God said we had to go on the next trip, which was in June of 2004.

So, we began to prepare in prayer for the trip, but you must understand something, this was against my nature. I was the church girl who sang in the choir, taught new believers in Sunday school for fifteen years or more, and was raised in a Pentecostal church for over twenty years. In all those years, I never said the word "missionary" and never ever thought about being one. I don't even think I ever asked God, "Do you want me to be a missionary?" Partly in fear that He would most definitely send me to a third world country, and not only would He send me, He would send me by myself. I do not think that it is a bad thing; I believe it was because I was not taught anything about missions in general. I was the one who would write a check to a visiting missionary, but don't ask me to go. Now I wish I would have gone when I was first saved. Now I want to go and can't get there fast enough. God was preparing my heart and life for a change for His use. This was part of His plan.

Preparation: The power and tugging of the Holy Spirit to change for His will, not ours.

Preparation: Prayer, word, direction

Preparation: Seek godly counsel.

Preparation: Listen to the inner person, the Holy Spirit.

Chapter 2

A RUSSIAN ORPHANAGE
Go.

Matthew 28:19–20 reads:

Go ye therefore, and teach all nations, baptizing them in the name of the Father, and of the Son, and of the Holy Ghost: Teaching them to observe all things whatsoever I have commanded you: and lo, I am with you always, even unto the end of the world.

Before you are sent out, there has to be a heart check. I knew that I had to stay humble before the throne of grace, making sure my heart was right before we left, and before we leave for future missions this must remain in my life, humbleness.

So we were going to go to Russia. All in God's good timing, Raul and I got on the plane, not knowing anyone. We were in a brand-new church, new city, newlyweds, and acting in absolute blind faith. We were ready to go on this adventure. We had all our "stuff"; it's funny now. It was a sixteen-hour flight, and I had never been out of California.

So if I can do it, you can do it. Truly, with God, all things are possible.

My first experience on the mission field was at Russian orphanages. The first two to three days there, I was sensitive to the surroundings, watchful, and cautious. That was all fine, but I don't think I was sensitive to what God really wanted to show me. It wasn't until days later that I began to really see the children and their hurts. I honestly hate to say this, but while there, I questioned if I really sincerely loved those orphans the way God the Father loved them. That made me sad. I really had to search my heart deeply and ask myself, "Do I love them the way Jesus does?"

As the days went on, I was finally able to say, "Okay, God, why am I here? What are You trying to say? I am open, I am listening, I want to see through Your eyes, God. I want to love the way You love." Almost immediately, things began to change. My heart was sensitive, and I began to feel a love that was so deep and different, something that I hadn't experienced in a long time. It was then that God began to speak and confirm what I already knew in my heart about missions. God said, "Yes, I want you to go," meaning that He was confirming His call or task for my life. He was drawing me closer to His heart by showing me His love for the orphans. This was all new to me. I had never been a missionary, so I really had no clue what it was like to go out and serve and love others in this way.

Matthew 28:19–20 took on a whole new meaning in my heart. I can honestly say this scripture is still in my heart and speaks with so much life and meaning. God knows you and I so intimately inside and out; He knows how to get your attention. He knows how many times He needs to speak to you until you get it. I just happen to be one of those daughters who needs a lot of reaffirming.

Part of my healing several years ago was Psalm 139. verse 3 says, "Thou compassest my path and my lying down, and art acquainted with all my ways." Verse 4 reads, "For there is not a word in my tongue, but, lo, O Lord, thou knowest it altogether."

So because He knows all about me, I am certain that He is reading every question or concern that is in my heart. I expect Him to answer, not that He will or always does, but I have seen and experienced some awesome answers by trusting the deep things of my heart to Him.

My friends, if you give God a chance to strengthen and develop those gifts that are already inside you, your entire Christian walk will be changed and on fire! Don't get me wrong; it is not all rosy, and you're not going to tiptoe through tulips. There will be change and challenges along your path.

It was in Russia where it all began for us. God moved in such awesome ways for Raul and I. I remember being on the plane at times thinking, *What in the world am I doing on this plane?* There was no turning back. God can and will confirm His calling wherever and whenever He chooses. If we hadn't been sensitive to His voice saying, "Go to Russia," we would have missed out. God forbid. So my question to you is, where are you right now? What plane are you on? Or what country is God calling you to? Maybe it is not out of the country where He is leading you but next door or a new city. Either way, my friend, you are called to serve our God. Move out of your comfort zone and get into the faith zone. You will never be the same.

To go back a bit to the next step of this journey, on the

plane we began to meet people. We met a woman, Joanie, and her two daughters. Raul and I connected with Joanie; she was like a spiritual mama for me. I love all the times when God has provided that type of women for me throughout my Christian walk. They have been so encouraging to my life. How I hope to be the same kind of godly woman to the young women the Lord brings my way.

Joanie was intuitive and sensitive to God's spirit. The first few days, she encouraged us, saying, "God is going to move quickly in your lives because you believe and have been calling out to Him. He hears you, He is going to answer you, and you know His voice." I remember thinking, *Oh, no, here it comes. We're going to a third world country for the rest of our lives.* I laugh about it now, not that there is anything wrong with the concept, definite preparation for that call!

One day we planned a play day for the children. Raul was cutting wood to make a platform for the day's event. I was by myself, walking across a large, beautiful, grassy plain where everyone else was hanging out. I happened to look to my left, and there was Joanie. She waved me over to her. As got closer to her, I felt the power of the Holy Spirit. By the time I to her, I began to weep. She knew what was happening and reached out to me. My head fell on her shoulder, and she held me. There were two other women there, and they laid their hands on me and began to pray. While they prayed, I heard my Lord's voice. He said, "You know what I am asking of you," and I replied, "Yes, Lord." Then He just loved me with His presence.

After that happened, Joanie looked at me and said, "You know, don't you?"

I said "Yes."

She asked, "What is it?"

"He is calling us to be missionary pastors to teach and help in the mission fields."

She said, "Yes, that is it."

Right then, Raul came over, and they prayed over us. That was the day the calling was confirmed; I will never forget that day.

If you seek Him, you will find Him when you seek with all your heart, soul, and strength. Matthew 7:7–8 says, "Ask and it shall be given you; seek and ye shall find, knock and it shall be opened unto you; for every one that asketh receiveth; and he that seeketh findeth; and to him that knocketh, it shall be opened." Amen. I will trust, rely, and depend on You and only You, God.

Don't be anxious; God will answer you. He will confirm the call upon your life in His own timing. There is nothing worse than feeling that God is not hearing your prayers, but He is. He's not worried about what He has called you to do. He is not worried about the timing. I can't tell you how many people that my husband and I have ministered to who think they messed up and that God would never use them. They once knew that there was a calling on their lives, but not anymore. Please do not ever think that way; this is a tragedy. God is big enough to take you, my friend, right where you are and redeem the time lost. He is bigger than lost time. Don't ever listen to that lie.

Sometimes the problem involves other people telling you that God can't use you because you have to work, how will you survive, it doesn't make sense that you want to go to China, or whatever the case may be. We have heard it all. But please use discernment when it comes to others having their inputs. Sometimes it's best not to say anything at all;

just wait on God. For myself, the voices were saying, "You can't do that, you can't go away from your family." Listen, in the end, God is the only voice in your life that should matter, when He says, "Go," He means, "Go!" He knows what is best for you. If you follow His voice, you will never go the wrong way. He will never lead you down the wrong path.

Let the challenge begin! Now we had to deal with the thoughts of going home and telling our families what happened in Russia.

Welcome home? Well not really. In fact, it wasn't that big a deal. My family was interested in how it went, and we shared some things that we saw and learned, but nothing really spiritual because my family is really not there. It's sad to say this, but I could not share the spiritual things we heard and saw. It wasn't until after several series of events—such as moving to Fontana, California, to live with my mom because she became ill in 2007—that Raul and I really began to share with the rest of the family that we felt called to become missionaries. But even then, the timing was not right. We began to go out on various medical mission trips in between work here and there.

After Russia, we served in Katrina with a medical relief organization that was founded by a dear friend we met in Moscow. We will never forget the day we met this tall, skinny guy. We thought this guy was a secret agent or something, but he turned out to be a new friend and brother, Read Taylor, who is still our dearest friend and brother.

Raul went to Thailand with Read and another brother in the Lord with hopes to establish a medical clinic in the north. For some reason, we were limited, but at least we stepped out and tried.

Then we went to Bolivia with a dear pastor and friend, Pastor Dan. There was also a chiropractor with us. We held a five-day medical clinic while Pastor Dan taught the Word; it was an awesome time. Pastor Dan laughs to this day because Raul and I don't speak Spanish very well, but while we were there, we were fluent. God opened our speech, and we were also able to understand what they said. So the people would line up and see the chiropractor, while Raul and I handed out medical supplies to the families. Then we prayed for the people, and God poured out His Spirit. People were crying when they left. We had the best time seeing God move in Bolivia. Praise be to our God.

Six months or so later, Raul went to Peru with medical supplies for a local clinic put on by a local church. The next year, we both went to Thailand; that trip was spiritually intense warfare. After Thailand, we kept seeking the Lord. I really thought that God would send us to South America. I honestly thought that Peru or Bolivia would be it.

On February 12, 2008, and October 30, 2010, my husband came to me with Isaiah 49:8–10. He said he felt God would be leading us to serve in Israel. *Israel? Really?* I thought. *I think he heard wrong.* That was until I read the scriptures in Isaiah 49. God confirmed something that He had spoken to me years ago, and my eyes were opened. How God? When? These questions are the beginnings of my missionary faith. That's what I like to call it—missionary faith. Every missionary whom I have spoken with has these same questions. I think God loves it because this is exactly where we need to be: running to Him with questions and seeking Him always.

I share all this with you so that you can see the journey

that God planned for us. I have taken you through a process of working out of our faith as we answered a call and said yes to the Lord. The questioning, the obedience, the wondering, the progress, the joy, and so forth. What a joy it is to serve our Lord, to see His love poured out on the poor, and to see His comfort in action. This is what I long for.

Chapter 3
HELP AND PROMISES
Be Strong—My Testimony

*Finally, my brethren, be strong in the Lord, and
in the power of his might.*

—Ephesians 6:10

As much as I want to jot down right where we are at this very moment, I can't because all the experiences that I have had are important for encouragement and field experience. Trust that what I am about to share with you will encourage you spiritually. We all have different experiences, but my hope is that these spiritual experiences will help you at some point. I also trust that the Lord will bring scripture to your remembrance and remind you of some of these spiritual victories. Our testimonies are powerful and must be shared to encourage others but always to glorify our Father God.

I know now that what God began in my life twenty-nine years ago, as painful as it was, would prepare me for this life mission.

At the age of twenty-four, I was diagnosed with a brain tumor. My sons were four and two and a half at the time. They are the joys of my life. Before the diagnosis, I knew that there was something wrong with me. I went to different doctors, and they could find nothing. Yet I was very sick. One doctor even said that I needed a shrink! I was a young believer at the time—only three years old in the faith—but I knew from the inside of my being that something was wrong. Always listen to your inner person, where the Holy Spirit dwells, as He is always right. You will need to hear His voice on the mission field.

Coming home from another doctor visit (the same doctor who said I needed a psychiatrist and gave me a prescription for Valium), I was so upset that I determined I was going to fast and pray because God knew what was wrong with me. I ripped up the prescription and threw it out the window, went home, got on my knees, and dedicated a fast. I said, "God, the doctors don't know what is wrong with me, but You do, so I am going to fast and pray until you tell me what it is."

During this time, my heart was racing erratically. I was having migraines so bad that I couldn't see or eat; I could not even hold down water it was so bad. I really think that I should have died because I had an incident with a migraine that lasted for four days. Neither food nor water stayed in my body for four days, so my family rushed me to the hospital emergency room. The doctor said it was allergies.

Right after this incident, I was okay for a few days. I ate, slept, and appeared to be okay. Then about two days later, I went to bed and had a grand mal seizure. I was rushed to the emergency room, where I lay in a semicoma for around six hours. When I woke up, the headache came back, and it was very painful. When I opened my eyes, my family was there, but I didn't know who they were. It was the strangest thing to ask them who they were. The good thing was that experience only lasted moments. Before I realized what was happening, it was over.

I had been going to church as usual and reading my Word, pressing into the Lord for help and holding onto His promises. I had the elders anoint me and pray for my healing.

James 5:13 says, "Is any sick among you? Let him call for the elders of the church; and let them pray over him, anointing him with oil in the name of the Lord." James 5:15 reads, "And the prayer of faith shall save the sick, and the Lord shall raise him up; and if he committed sins, they shall be forgiven."

So I did exactly what the Word said to do, believe that God knew and heard me. While in the emergency room, I had an experience that I will never forget. My grandma Vagle was there. She was my spiritual mentor and taught me the Word and so much more. (She is now with the Lord.) When I opened my eyes, she was praying over me, saying, "The blood of Jesus," over and over. It was awesome. Other family members were there, but as I said earlier, and it is funny now, when I looked at them, I did not know who they were. They were saying, "We are your family," and I remember saying, "I don't know you." Then it came back to me who they were.

Anyway, my family explained that I had a grand mal seizure and that the doctors were running tests. I remember asking for something for my headache, and the nurse walked out to get me some medication. They had already run a CAT scan of my brain, took blood, and so on. Then I heard the doctor walking toward my room; it was like time stood still. My family members didn't move or say a word. The doctor stopped in his tracks, and just then, the Holy Spirit came in the room and said, "You have a brain tumor, but it is not cancer, and you are not going to die."

The minute I said okay, He left and all was back to normal. Right after, the doctor walked in, tapped me on the leg and said, "Well you have a brain tumor, but I am 99 percent positive that it is not cancer, and you are going to be fine."

I had the news before the doctor told me, and the doctor used almost the same words as the Holy Spirit. After a while, I was sent home to prepare for surgery.

My family took the news hard; my father, mother, and brothers all came to the Lord through this event. The day I went to a doctor's appointment that would begin the preparation process for surgery, I came out of the doctor's office to see one of my brothers, standing there and crying. I said, "Mario, it's okay. God said that I was going to live and not die." I comforted him as much as I could. It's pretty amazing when you're in this kind of situation how God will step in and carry you. It's really very powerful how protective God is.

The doctors sent me home to prepare for seventeen days. As I look back, I see the greatness of my Lord Jesus, His care, love, and comfort over me. I was home resting, taking care of my sons, going to church, and still going down to be anointed and prayed over. As I pressed into the Lord during the waiting time, waves of doubt would come over me. It was like a voice that said, "What if God didn't say that you were going to live? Maybe you are going to die!" Then fear would try to grip me. I would go to prayer, ask God to help me, and hold onto His promises. Isaiah 41:10 tells us, "Fear thou not, for I am with thee, be not dismayed for I am thy God, I will help thee, I will uphold thee with the right hand of my righteousness." I prayed this verse over and over, until the peace of God comforted me.

One night I went to bed and had a visitation. He was my angel; he had to be. He was the most beautiful being I have ever seen. He was huge; his wings were huge. He was strong and as tall as the ceiling. He stood at my bedside, staring at me with one hand on his chin, like he was thinking. His head was a little tilted, and he was smiling. I remember smiling at him and I mentally asked, *What?*

He pointed his finger at me and said, "By faith, by faith, by faith." He must have said this over one hundred times.

Then I said, "I get it." He had the biggest smile and left.

When I woke up, I got on my knees and prayed. I felt the Lord say, "From this moment on, you will live by faith, walk by faith, talk by faith; your entire life is to be by faith." At the time, I thought I knew what He was talking about, but I know now that I did not know nearly enough about living by faith. I had and have so much to learn.

The same week, I had another visitation. But this time it was not an angel; it was a demon. Yes, he came to kill me; it was a spirit being ugly. He jumped on me and started choking me. I was in the spirit, so I couldn't fight him off. I remember feeling such fear, but the minute that I was able to say, "Jesus," it left. I believe it was God showing me the two spiritual beings that are real.

What does this have to do with preparation? I believe that this has everything to do with preparation because the Word of God says in Ephesians 6:12, "For we wrestle not against flesh and blood, but against principalities, against powers, against the rulers of the darkness of this world, against spiritual wickedness in high places."

When you travel to foreign countries, you can count on spiritual attacks. Ephesians 6:10–18 instructs us to put on the whole armor of God. You put it on by faith, in confidence, knowing that the enemy is defeated. If God is for us, who can be against us? Be confident that nothing can separate us from the love of God through Christ Jesus, Amen. I will trust, rely, and depend on You and only You, God.

Getting ready for the surgery, I was ready. People prayed day and night, and fasted. The day of the surgery came, and I dropped my sons off at my sister-in-law's. It was hard for me to walk away. It was December 17, 1984.

When I awoke after surgery, my dad stood next to the bed with a nurse. The nurse said, "Christine, wake up."

I woke up as much as possible, but I was heavily sedated. My dad said, "I'm here mija."

I said, "Okay, Dad."

The nurse had me move my hands and feet. Then she said to my dad, "She's going to be fine," and walked away. I dozed off back to sleep.

To make a long story short, I was fine and had no pain. The doctors were amazed at my recovery. I am still amazed at my recovery. All these years later, I am amazed at God's keeping power.

A miracle happened that night for a young man who had come in several times before with brain aneurysms. This time was supposed to be his last, but God saved him that night. It was truly a miracle. A nurse told me all the details. I remember praying for this man right after he came in. I asked him what was wrong with him, and he told me that he kept having aneurysms and that this was the last surgery they could do.

I said, "Well, it is going to be the last surgery because God is going to heal you." I reached out my hand to hold his hands and pray for him. The Holy Spirit came in that room so strong he wept and wept. I asked, "Do you believe that God can heal you?"

He said, "Yes."

I said, "You will be healed." Then I went back to sleep.

The same nurse who worked on my surgery worked on him. She came into my room and gave me the details of his surgery. She said that they opened him up at the base of the neck, looking for a certain color fluid. It wasn't there, so the doctor said, "Sew him up. There's nothing more we can do."

She said, "I don't know why, but I said, 'Try a half inch lower.' The doctor did and found the fluid they were looking for. This saved his life."

Praise God for such a miracle of life all the way around; He is wonderful. More than wonderful. That same nurse said that I should not have lived through my surgery. She had seen many surgeries like mine, and those patients either died or had to learn to walk and talk all over again. Some were even paralyzed on one side. She went on to say that my surgery was different; it went so smoothly, and everything was as it was supposed to be. My miracle was that I had no side effects, no pain, no paralysis. I told her that it was because of God and because I prepared through prayer. Other people fasted and prayed for me. I also told her that God said I would live and not die.

She believed every word. I asked her if she went to church. She said no but that she wanted to and would do so. I told her to commit to Jesus and that He would do awesome things with her life.

The next few days I was up and about. I was never in my room; I went around praying for the sick and leading people to Christ. It was amazing. My doctors and nurses would page me to come to my room so they could check my head, stitches, and give me my pain medicine. But I would tell the nurse, "I don't need pain medicine 'cause I am not in pain."

She said, "That's impossible."

I said, "No, it's not. It's God."

She shook her head and walked away, smiling. I found out that this nurse was a backslider, so I ministered to her and told her to get back to church. She didn't say one way or the other, but she heard me.

My doctor came in early one morning so that he could release me because, he said, I was never in my room anyway. Praise God for His loving kindness. I was home on Christmas Eve 1984.

The rest is the healing and restoration of my soul that came from the Lord's Word and through prayer. I went home healed and am still healed. Preparation runs deep. There is so much that God needs to do in my life before I can be effective in a foreign land. Please let Him work things in and out of your life so that you will be prosperous and successful wherever He sends you. The whole purpose is so that Christ in you and the hope of glory can shine through your life. That is our testimonies. Testimonies come out of darkness such as trials and possible hopeless situations. John 3:30 says, "He must increase and I must decrease."

There have been many trials, struggles, good times, and bad times, and they caused me to run to Him for help. So when we are sent out onto the mission field, we will know and be ready for any spiritual attack or experience that may come. Hold onto God's promises for your mission. If you make a list, include the many promises that God has given to you.

Hold on to them. Cry out to God for help; He will meet you right where you are right now.

There is a spiritual battle going on as we read in Ephesians 6. When we find ourselves in any form of trouble, we are instructed to cry out to the Father, who hears us and who will deliver us. Psalm 3:3 says, "But you, O Lord, are a shield for me, my glory and the one who lifts up my head."

Friend, you will be tested and tried along the way and years before God sends you out. All so that you know Him and His love and power! Expect some bumpy roads on the way to the mission field or wherever God leads you. We are constantly learning and growing in our faith walk, and the entire point is to cry out to God. It is important to always give God a chance to respond; a lot of times we pray and expect an immediate answer. We never give God a chance to respond, thus missing out on God showing up. You may miss a miracle answer. Always remember to wait on God; you will never be sorry. It brings God joy to answer His children.

The next experience I share is one of my favorites. Timmie, a neighbor-friend of our family was sick and dying of cancer. She was at home in bed, waiting to die. One day I was visiting my mom, and she told me that Timmie was dying of cancer. It really made me sad.

I said to my mother, "Oh, I really need to see her." I remember vividly that it was a Friday. I went home and fasted Saturday and Sunday and read Isaiah 58. That chapter is such an inspiration of a perfect fast from our loving Father.

On Monday, I went to see Timmie. My heart pounded as I walked up to knock on the door. As I did, I knew God was with me in such a strong way. I was amazed at His showing up. Psalm 118 says, "it is the right hand of God that moves valiantly." When He saves, He saves.

Cindy, Timmie's daughter, opened the door and said, "Hi, Tina."

"Hi, Cindy. I came to see your mom."

"Oh, she is so sick, I don't think you should see her." I was thinking, *Oh no*, when Cindy said, "Why don't you come in for a while?" I quickly said okay and went in. I walked in the living room and sat down and talked with Cindy and her dad.

As we chatted, I said, "Oh, so she is too sick for me to see her today?" I said this, trying to make it happen.

Mr. Simmons, Timmie's husband, said, "Yes, she is too sick. You can't see her."

I prayed in the Spirit while he talked away. I prayed, *Okay, God, I know you sent me today.* Just then, and I don't know how to explain this except God opened my eyes to see this, I saw black shadows fly directly over his head. Then I saw a bright light, and angels were fighting directly over his head. It was amazing. I tried not to stare, afraid he would think I was crazy. It all happened in an instant, and then it was gone. I knew exactly what it was.

We continued our conversation, and it was done, the fight was over. God sent me to lead Timmie to salvation, and He fought the battle. I know now that the battle started when I began to fast and pray. And when I knocked on the door, it was on! The supernatural was set in motion. God showed up and won.

Just then, Mr. Simmons said, "You know, I think you can see her. Go ahead, and go on in."

Cindy and I walked in the room. Cindy said, "Mom, Tina is here to see you."

She asked, "Who?"

"Tina is here. Our neighbor."

"Oh, yes. Please have her come in."

I walked in where she lay, fragile. I noticed that she had a statue of the Virgin Mary at the foot of her bed. "Hi, Timmie. How are you today?"

"I am in so much pain," she replied.

I said, "Okay, well I came to pray for you."

She said, "What?"

"I came to pray for you."

"Okay, please do."

"Have you been praying?"

She answered, "Yes, I have been saying, 'God please, please help me.'"

I said, "Well, God has heard your prayers and has sent me to pray for you. Do you believe that God has sent me?"

She said, "Yes, yes." I asked her this because I wanted to see where her faith level was.

"Good. We need to give your heart to Jesus. Are you ready to do this?"

She said, "Yes." So Timmie accepted the Lord Jesus, and He was immediately present in her room. I laid hands on her, and the pain left. She almost jumped out of her bed. "The pain, it's gone. It left," she said.

I said, "Praise God, Timmie. He loves you so much."

I stayed quite a while with her. She had a little TV in her room, and I changed the channel to the Christian station and moved the statue. I told her to listen to this station to learn about Jesus. She said she would, and she was so thankful. I left to let her rest, and God stayed to keep her.

The next day I went to see her. I walked in the room,

and it was so bright with His presence. And so was her countenance. I just smiled; she was completely touched by God. We chatted a bit, and I prayed for her. Then I said, "Well, you don't need me anymore. God is here. He will take care of you now." I kissed her and left.

At church during worship, I asked the Lord if He wanted me to go back, and He said no. The next week, He took her home. Later that week, I had a dream or vision. I saw her in a white robe, dancing free before the Lord. It was done, mission accomplished.

Our lives belong to the Lord to do His will. If we are connected to God by the Holy Spirit, we have full access to the supernatural throne of grace to bring life, healing, and hope to others. But most of all, we are to bring salvation, the good news of Jesus Christ. God will always help us, and He will always provide His promises to us through His Word.

Lastly, when I was thirty-one years old, I came down with chicken pox. I packed a bag and went home to my parents so that they could take care of me. After the third night, I was pretty ill. I told my mom that I felt like I was going to die that night. She broke down and cried. Then we both got on our knees and prayed. Well, that night I believe I did die; I went straight into the Lord's presence in heaven. It was so beautiful. I was on green hills; there was a crystal-clear lake. I wore a white gown, and the Lord was walking in front of me ("He leads me beside still waters"). I was skipping free, whole, healthy, happy behind Him. The second I thought, *I don't want to go back*, He turned around and smiled at me, and I was back in my body. I woke up and told my mom all that happened. We wept, got on our knees, and prayed.

You can count on Him to show up in your mission fields. He will show up on your behalf and on behalf of those to whom He sends you. Listen to the Holy Spirit; He will tell you what to do and say.

Chapter 4
LEAD ME

He leads me beside the still waters.

—Psalm 23

Preparation to serve takes a lifetime. It is a continuous process. There are so many issues in our lives that need to be addressed by God, but He is more than able to clean us up little by little.

I also learned that God will take care of some things here and some there, meaning monetarily and personally. I do know that God cannot use a clogged heart or a distracted life. So given the process, I wouldn't have it any other way, as uncomfortable as it may be. Being in a relationship with our Lord means He has full permission and authority to mess up our lives. Yes, mess them up—all for good of course. However, these times are hard because He gets into the cracks and areas of our hearts and begins to clean house.

Not too long ago, the Lord revealed something that I had been carrying in my heart from years ago. It had to do with a past relationship and hurts. At a family gathering, I overheard something and got upset. The next day in church, during worship, I felt the Lord say to my heart, *He maketh me to lie down in green pastures, He leads me beside still waters, He restores my soul.* Needless to say, I was broken and humbled before my Lord and began to search my heart.

As I searched, I asked the Lord to show me all that needed to come out of my heart and to wash the heartache away. We all need cleaning from time to time, but it would really benefit us to keep in mind that God desires continual cleaning. This is our relationship with Him, allowing cleaning of our hearts and minds. This will go on until Jesus comes back.

As I began to study Psalm 23, the Lord began to speak ever so clearly. First, He showed me the part of my heart that was sick. I felt Him say, *Why do you get so worked up about this past issue? I am the Good Shepherd, who leads you into green pastures. I will tenderly lead you; your enemy will push you and drag you uncomfortably into tough paths and will always bring up your past.*

I was gently led into being cleansed of this hurt. I had to let it go. That is when the Lord showed me that He cannot move or produce good fruit when a heart is clogged by past hurts. You and I must constantly be cleansed of whatever they are.

Have you ever seen sheep grazing on green pastures? They don't have a care in this world; they are chewing and chewing in peace. That is what our heavenly Father wants from us—to graze on the green pastures of His Word, graze in peace, and chew on His Word.

The Lord had me study this chapter. Verse 1 says: "The Lord is my shepherd, I shall not want." What a timely scripture to speak to my heart, to clean my heart, and to increase my faith. As I pondered this verse, I began to speak it out loud to hear myself proclaim, "The Lord is *my* shepherd, I shall not want!"

As I did this, I became peaceful and rested inside my soul, causing me to trust that He is able to heal my hurts and past mistakes. "The Lord is my shepherd, I shall not want"; I trust You, God, for healing, deliverance, for provisions, for all that we need to do Your will and good works in Israel. I trust You that the fruit that You will produce will remain.

Once again, I have seen His love and supernatural power. Now all I need to do is rest and trust in His leading. I am learning that as He leads, He cleans. He wants more of our hearts, and He deserves all and more than we can give. Romans 12:1 says, "this is our reasonable service, I choose to give my heart wholly to be cleansed and changed by His Holy Spirit and by His Word."

Verse 2 of Psalm 23 says, "He leads me beside the still waters." God began to show me how He had been trying to help me and heal me, but He had to cause me to be still so that He could speak to me. It just happened to be during worship that I heard Him speak and come to my rescue. I was broken, and that is where God meets us, when we are broken and emptied. Since that day, I have pondered these verses quietly, and once again, He confirmed His voice to me through worship. A song, "The Lord Is My Shepherd," came on by an artist that we love. It is so beautiful it takes me to that place with the Lord.

Being led to still waters is so powerful for our walk because it shows you and me His divine leadership. He so desires to lead us by the hand. I like to picture Him leading with His staff, gently walking before me. He leads me beside the still waters.

I was recently asked how the Holy Spirit bears witness with my conscience. As I thought about it, I had to answer that in quietness, this is true. I have learned that for me to hear God's leading, I have to be quiet and be in a quiet place. For me, too many words or too much talking is a waste of time and most of the time, not profitable. Try this test. When you are among your family and friends, try being quiet and listen only to all the words spoken. You will be surprised at your findings. The Holy Spirit gave me this test to do years ago, and it still stands true. It is hard to be still and listen.

"What a Friend We Have in Jesus" is an old hymn that we used to sing. What a privilege to carry everything to God in prayer. We seldom do, though prayer is the key to being led by the Lord. Never lay down your most important weapon of prayer! Prayer is your lifeline. It is your fellowship with God. It is where you get instruction and leading for your life and ministry.

Take everything to God in prayer, always. He is our Good Shepherd, who leads us through our journeys of life and serving. Then He leads us onto eternity unto Himself. In this life now, God is our divine leader, who will lead us when we are in difficult places and being tested.

Deuteronomy 8:2 reads, "And thou shalt remember all the ways which the Lord thy God led thee these forty years in the wilderness, to humble thee, and to prove thee, to know what was in thine heart, whether thou wouldest keep his commandments or no." This is a great scripture to consider and meditate on when in a difficult spot. This scripture is true. I remember a pastor once saying that as believers, we must be confident in our Lord, keep His Word in our hearts, and be faithful to His Word.

Tough times are testing indeed, especially when you have made up your mind that you are going to follow God's plan for your life, and you want to go for the Great Commission.

Things will get tough and heated. Will we be faithful when we are in the desert places? Times when you need provisions, times when you are far away from home and feel lonely? Praise God for our great Shepherd.

Psalm 77:20 tells us, "Thou leddest thy people like a flock by the hand of Moses and Aaron." There is no place that God cannot reach you and lead you to and from, ever. In Psalm 139:9–10, we find, "If I take the wings of the morning, and dwell in the uttermost parts of the sea; Even there shall thy hand lead me, and thy right hand shall hold me." What great comfort we can take in our Lord's Word.

I think my issue with mission work was security. How would we pay our bills? We can trust in God's leading day to day, week to week, month to month. He delights in us running to him, crying out, "Abba Father, help us." Have I got it all together? No! I am still running to Him.

May He lead us beside still waters; be still and hear His leading. There are benefits to allowing Him to lead us. He will forever lead you to green pastures, beside still waters to drink of living waters (John 7:37–38). When we drink of the living waters, we have the stillness of soul and satisfaction.

One of my favorite scriptures is John 10:22: "My sheep hear my voice and I know them and they follow me." God does not want us wandering aimlessly like sheep without a shepherd. The Lord is my Shepherd, I will want for nothing; He provides for me, protects me, leads me, and stays with me even when going through the valley of the shadow of death. We have this guarantee that when we find ourselves not in green pastures, His gentle, still voice will break through the distractions and say, "I am the Good Shepherd. Follow me; I will lead you to rest in green pastures. Feed on my Word and rest."

This is all part of preparation—getting our hearts unclogged, allowing Him to cleanse our hearts and souls with His precious Word and prayer. Why? So He can prepare you and me for the mission field ministry. And so He can use us to bring salvation, hope, healing, and restoration to those to whom He will send you and me.

Let's talk about verse 3: "He restores my soul." This is one of my favorite verses because I lived and continue to live this verse. Preparation comes through restoration, and restoration comes through His Word, prayer, and love. Several experiences led me to now. Right now, at this moment, my restoration comes through Psalm 23:1–3.

Amazing love is His plan to restore our souls and lead us in the paths of righteousness for His namesake. What does, "He restoreth my soul," mean in verse 3? Well, I have learned through many mental trials and tribulations that perfect restoration comes through the Word and prayer. Our souls consist of our minds, emotions, and wills. Our souls belong to God, and since they do, it is our responsibility to keep our souls whole and healthy.

As a young woman in my early twenties, I was in a relationship that was mentally and emotionally abusive. My soul was sick and unhealthy, and this made me physically sick. I knew that I had to do something, or I would eventually die. I just knew it. At my church fellowship, I engulfed myself in prayer and Bible studies, and my own devotion became intense. God healed me, encouraged me, and taught me how He sees me through His Word. So I want to encourage you to be whole in your soul. Press into the Word of God, and pray for healing. If there is something that you may be struggling with, have the elders pray for you. I am so thankful to the Lord for always having godly elders in my life who prayed for and loved me, never judging. This is vital to your calling to the mission field as you will be at some point mentally and emotionally challenged.

"He leads me in the paths righteousness for His namesake." Years ago, my pastor was praying for me and he said, "Don't worry. God will lead you and guide you always, and He will be your rear guard." Well here it is, years later, and more and more I am seeing this very thing come to pass in my life. I am finding that my spiritual eyes are opened, and I am able to see His hand going before my paths.

I like how the Word says, "paths of righteousness." You will find that God has many paths of righteousness for us to travel on. And rest assured, He is on every one for His namesake. For me, this means He will never fail me. This is fresh and exciting for me. It should be for all of us. I believe that God is alive and wants to do fresh and exciting things in and through all of us. I don't want to be so mature I miss the things that God wants to do fresh and new in my life. May we never lose zeal, passion, and the freshness of God.

Maybe you are dry right now or have lost your zeal or passion. Well, my friend, run to Him; ask Him to fill you afresh with the power, joy, and love of the Holy Spirit. Run to Him crying, broken, humble in spirit. Come to Him to be restored. If you're angry, tell Him. He is not surprised at your state. Come to Him kicking and screaming. Come to Him with questions. It's okay; He knows all about it anyway. Remember, He is your Father: "You are of God little children" (1 John 4:6).

"God, I think we are ready to go."

"No, dear child, not so fast."

Sound familiar?

Chapter 5

GUIDE ME

I will instruct thee and teach thee in the way which thou shalt go, I will guide thee with mine eye.

—*Psalm 32:8*

I find this chapter so wonderful and encouraging because this is exactly where we are right now in the preparation process. I find myself crying out in the night hours, "Oh, God, please guide us on this path." For me, the guidance process comes along with all the questions that totally mess me up at times. It is during this process that I wish I was quicker to get to the point. Because I am not, I am learning to try not to figure things out. It can become frustrating, but it is necessary for preparation as I am learning so much, including that I had a problem with trust.

This may sound elementary to some, but even though I've always known that God would lead, guide, and provide for me, this is different as now God asks me to let go so that I can grow and so that He can show Himself to me in a new way. You see, I have always had to have a plan to survive. My thoughts were that God's leading, guiding, and provisions would always be tangible, something that I could see on paper.

I blame this partly on lack of my understanding of Gods word at the time. This led me to believe the Word of God in a completely different context. Since then—and now for ten plus years being properly taught the Word line for line, precept for precept—I see God's Word come alive fresh and new. This is how God prepares you and guide you for service. Any service through His Word builds the foundation you will stand on as you venture out in life and ministry/mission fields.

Every once in a while, my "Pentecostalness" will pop up. Not to say that it's wrong to show emotion toward the Lord, but the Word clearly says to shout unto the Lord with a voice of triumph, and sing unto the Lord a new song. Sometimes I think this is lacking in some fellowships. I truly thank my husband for being patient and loving toward me as he sat with me and taught and showed me the right way to study God's Word. Not to mention Pastor Frank Sanchez and Pastor Dan Finfrock, who God brought into my life. They are good, godly teachers and preachers; I love these guys. As one of my favorite pastors, Dan says, "We are to feed on green grass, green pastures."

I must say that I miss the altar, or as my soul brothers and sisters would say, "Doing business with God at the altar." The times at the altar were my times with God, where I met with Him and left assured and strengthened, not based on feeling there were times of feeling nothing at all, but knowing that He was there, leading and guiding me every moment one day at a time. For me, seeking God's guidance has been a great time of pressing into His Word and being assured that

He hears my prayers and will answer in His time. Take time to seek guidance. Don't rush; let His Word go before you.

As I write this, I am practicing listening to His voice, crying out in the night hours, "God, please continue to guide us." It may be redundant, but I can't express enough how important it is to continually cry out to God. At this very time, I am in a new place of trusting in His Word and in His Holy Spirit to "guide me onto pleasant places" (Psalm 23:2), "guide me in decision making" (Psalm 25:19), "guide me in the midst of uncertainties (Isaiah 42:16), "guide me by wise counsel" (Psalm 73:24), and "one day He will Guide me unto the end of my life" (Psalm 48:14) for this God is our God forever and ever.

The awesomeness of preparation is this: because He loves us, He gives us this amazing opportunity to know Him deeper and deeper, all for His glory and for our benefit in heaven.

Guidance for new things is exciting for me. It causes me to be still and causes discipline, obedience, and action. Guidance by the Holy Spirit causes challenge; it's like taking a break and taking a breath of fresh air on race day. If you've ever been on a track team, you prepare yourself physically; you do breathing exercises. It's the same thing for me when I feel God guiding me onto new grounds of ministry. Take a breath, and get ready. It's like God saying, "Look I have a new present for you that is going to grow you and stretch you."

I wrote two dates in my Bible at Isaiah 42. The first is 1-18-85; the second is12-3-13. The book of Isaiah is one of my favorites, along with Psalms and the Gospels. Lately, I have been reading this chapter again and again with the hope of this promise that new things are coming. I know this chapter refers to becoming a new creation in Christ, but I also associate the following verse with God doing new things in my life and yours, "Behold the former things are come to pass, and new things do I declare; before they spring forth I tell you of them" (Isaiah 42:9). Chapter 42 also has great meaning in my life. When I would read this, I never really understood that God was speaking about Christ, who His Son, and the calling of Christ duties to the Jews first and then to the Gentiles. As I read this chapter, I wondered, *How in the world does this apply to me?* I was taught differently by my mentors in the early years of my salvation, but now I can see now how it applies, especially since we have been called to serve in Israel.

God's guidance in my earlier years led me to a strong foundation. I mentioned in chapter 4 how I was in turmoil both mentally and emotionally, and God healed my soul.

One of the requirements was that at the end of the training classes, the students were to go on a mission trip to Israel. That's the other miracle—provisions for one month. So we began to pray, and my husband began to meet with some pastors, sharing that God was calling us to Israel. We began to ask for support.

One day we were driving home from class, and my husband got a phone call from a mission pastor. He said they received an unusual donation earmarked for Israel and that they didn't know what to do with it, until the congregational pastor told them he had heard about our trip. Well, when we got the check, it was exactly what we needed for our apartment for one month. The airfare was all paid for by air miles, and we only had to pay the difference of four hundred dollars. So with that, we knew that God had called us to go in January 2014.

Now that it was all clear, we had to prepare to leave the business. I admit this was and still is tough on me. However, through a series of events, we left the business and went to Israel for one month. It's funny to me now, but at the time, I was waking up at night saying, "God, we can't do this. We can't leave our business." God would immediately speak to me and say, "Just give me a month."

Then I would be okay. But then I would wake up again and say, "God, I can't do this. Raul can go, and I will stay and run the business." That is *not* what God said to do. We were to both go on this trip. Then I would be okay again, but then I would cry out to Him again, and He would immediately speak to me, telling me to be patient and trust Him. He said, "Nothing is set in stone. Just give me a month. And just wait until you get there. Haven't I said in My Word that I will instruct you, lead you, and guide you?"

That was it, no more struggle. I knew that this was set in heaven, and there was no turning back. Once God sets your destination in heaven, there is no turning back; you are going. He will give you every encouragement along the way with confirmations. Everything around you will point to the fact that you are going, and you will know that God has written this in heaven for you to do. And only you can do it. Don't resist by questioning or delaying, just obey. With obedience, He is pleased.

There are miracles along the way as you allow God to guide you. Once we arrived in Israel, we settled in, and the first week I got sick. I was down for about four days. Then we began to walk and pray. God gave us very specific instructions to walk and pray in a certain city. So that is what we did. But there were distractions asking us to do certain things, but God said to stick to His plan, so we did.

It was a powerful time of fasting and praying for a city. God had plans for this city. On the second week, we were informed that there was a fellowship there, so we contacted the pastor. As I got the address, I realized that their facility was literally half a block from our apartment. We had no knowledge of this city at all, but God did. We met the pastor at the midweek services and served at their Thursday night outreach to the poor. Once the pastor got to know us better, a kinship formed among us, and it was refreshing. Where God leads you, He will guide you, and you will see answers if you allow and are sensitive to hearing Him.

New Things

As we were in the preparation of going on this trip, I kept hearing in the Spirit, "New things, new things." As I prayed, I didn't question. I just said, "Lord, please help me to be sensitive to the new things that You want to do. I don't want to miss anything that You have for us to do in Israel." With expectant hearts, we prayed intently and were open to what the Lord wanted to do while we were there. There were days when we didn't go anywhere; we just stayed in and prayed, read the Word, and waited for His guidance for the next day. When He did speak, He guided us to new people whom we were able to share with. We asked the Lord to lead us and guide us so that we could be effective each day. That is what God looks for: vessels who are willing to follow His lead and guidance each day. I remember wondering, *When was the last time that I actually had time to sit before the Lord and just talk to Him and read His word quietly, and just sit in His presence?*

It reminded me of the book of Acts. Paul went to the beach to pray, and a woman heard him praying, heeded his words, and became a believer. Those are the kinds of appointments that happen when you allow God to guide your steps, remembering that He writes the pages of your life in Christ. Praise God for His loving staff that leads us, guides us, and corrects us. Here are a couple of reminders about you and me.

1. You have purpose, the call of God, the Fruit of the Spirit.
2. Make preparation through prayer, the Word of God, and godly counsel.
3. Allow His direction, leading, and guidance,

Chapter 6

HIDE ME

He that dwelleth in the secret place of the most High shall abide under the shadow of the Almighty.

—Psalm 91:1

Our first week in Israel, we got word from home that our business lost a good-sized job. Not happy—abide!

The first week I also got sick with bronchitis. Not happy—abide!

The second week, our business had little money to buy materials. Distracted and not happy—abide!

Then the thought began to run through my mind that I needed to go home and get this handled as soon as possible. Then the Lord began to speak to me about obedience and letting go. But how could I let go when our business was falling apart?

I thought, *I mean, after all God, You allowed us to have a business. Don't You care? What is going on?* God never promised us a rose garden along the way. In fact, serving requires desert and warfare experiences like this, and we all know that financial troubles are the worst. It is important to remember that God allows these desert times in our lives because it causes us to run to Him, and it causes me to hide under His shadow. For me, the desert preparations of my life are usually used to bring death to my flesh. I am learning that when the provisions are dry, I must seek His Word for instruction and direction. As I write this chapter, I find that we are in this position of seeking, stretching, and hiding under His shadow. We can do nothing for ourselves. Our hopes must be in Jesus, for all and in all.

I am learning that my flesh reacts with all of the whys when looking and trying to make things happen. I laugh because, "making it happen," has been my life. I had to survive in my earlier years, so making it happen was my drive. I always kept my heart in check with God, but if I could move things around to accomplish something, I did. However, God has been forever changing all this for the purpose of preparation for the Israel mission fields. I just know that He works all these things in our lives for His purpose. Through our trials and tests, He pulls us closer and deeper. I rest in the fact that I hear His voice; I want to be still enough to always hear His voice. I also know that when my soul cries out in the night hours, He is pleased.

After we returned from Israel, we immediately jumped back into working the business only to find it upside down financially. Not fun, not happy—abide! It was as if a bomb went off in our business. We literally had no work and no cash flow. We began to seek the Lord and once again cried out, "God, heal the business. This is our tent-making that pays our bills. How could this happen to us? We did what You asked us to do, God! Abide!

As we went through everything, we noticed that it would

be easier to not have the business and only work to make the money necessary to live. The biggest bills are for the business, but it also provides for our employees and their families. Again, here is my flesh reasoning with what I think needs to be done. Again, the Spirit began to speak to me, telling me to just let go and come to Him.

One morning as I awoke and began to get ready to go to the office, a song came up in my soul. It is called "Break Every Chain." I saw myself in the office, playing this song over and over. I saw this song going up in heaven to break every chain that has been over the business and cash flow. I couldn't wait to get to the office so that I could begin warfare.

Yes, I played the song over and over again. I sang and prayed in the Spirit. I did this over and over for weeks. Then we began to see breakthroughs. Work began to come in, and cash flow began to come forth. Of course, the cash flow comes and goes, but in all this, the Lord teaches us that He will always provide what we need. I have had a problem with only what I have need of I'm certain it's because of security, who doesn't want security, but God requires Faith. However, I am coming to understand that when we are on the mission field, we will be living, walking, and trusting in Him and Him alone. I am sure that Paul didn't have a rolling bank account that He trusted in. I am learning and growing.

Again, it's all about Jesus. Jesus said in John 15:4, "Abide in me, and I in you. As the branch cannot bear fruit of itself, unless it abides in the vine, neither can you, unless you abide in me." To abide in Him is a lifetime experience of change going on our inner selves so that we bring forth fruit that will remain.

Verse 5 goes on to say, "I am the vine, you are the

branches, He who abides in Me, and I in him bears much fruit; for without me you can do nothing." It should be the desire of our hearts to bear spiritual fruit. The spiritual fruit of the Lord begins in our hearts, and the fruit of life and the fruits of the spirit then pour onto others freely.

When you dwell in the secret place of the Most High, you abide under His shadow. How do you dwell in the secret place? When you sing praise to Him, you are dwelling. When you are in your devotional time, you are dwelling. When you take a walk with the Lord in the morning or evening, you are dwelling and abiding. When you are alone in your office and begin to cry aloud, you are abiding and hiding under the shadow of the Almighty. This is the safest place to be.

Psalm 91:2 "I will say of the Lord, He is my refuge and my fortress: my God, in Him will I trust. Surely he shall deliver thee from the snare of the fowler, and from the noisome pestilence." When we came home from Israel, we came home to noisome pestilence. Remember, we are in continual spiritual warfare, and our enemy shows no mercy. His tactics are sly and devious. The thief cometh to steal, kill, and destroy. So yes, of course we came home to a fierce battle to destroy us. You will experience these types of attacks, so be prepared to go into battle, always remembering that He will deliver you from every evil attack.

Praise God for His faithfulness to deliver us from every evil work. Psalm 91 is so full of God's promises for protection and reassurances that evil will never overtake His own: "He shall cover thee with His feathers, and under His wings shalt thou trust: His truth shall be thy shield and buckler."

During this period, through all my quiet time with the Lord, I kept hearing Him say, "Just be still." Now I know what He was doing; He was fighting the battle as I was being still. I am sensitive to the Spirit; over and over I heard Him say, "Be still, be still." I was hiding under the shadow while He was fighting. That is what you and I are supposed to do, nothing less. He is the God of battles, so be encouraged if you are in a raging battle. He is with you. He will hide you if you abide in Him. Here is a promise for you and me: Psalm 91:5, "Thou shalt not be afraid for the terror by night; nor for the arrow that flieth by day." We can boast in the keeping power of God. Regardless of any physical, emotional, or financial battles that surround us, the Lord Himself is our refuge and very present help in any kind of trouble.

Psalm 36:5–7 reads,

> *Thy mercy O Lord is in the heavens; and thy faithfulness reacheth unto the clouds. Thy righteousness is like the great mountains; thy judgments are a great deep: O Lord, thou preservest man, and beast. How excellent is thy lovingkindness, O God! Therefore the children of men put their trust under the shadow of thy wings.*

I have learned through this time to walk quietly and to search my heart again, asking the Lord for wisdom as to what direction He was leading us concerning the business. "Oh, God, please hide me in your direction." After a few months of working hard and lots of prayers, we began to see the Lord bring healing to the business. He was literally providing only what we needed. I began to hear the Lord say to downsize. But where do we downsize? Within a few days, I began to really notice that our office rent was something that we could do without. So we began to pray about the office. Then, after three months, we decided to let the office go. That was one step. Then we moved on to some vendors to whom we owed money. "Oh, God, please hide us in your provision. We need your help."

We sometimes need to hire other professionals to get certain jobs done. We began to notice that our finances were not stretching to cover all the needs to be covered. That is when we continually cry out, "God, please hide us through this."

I don't mean, "Hide us so that this will go away." I mean, "Hide us so that we can be safe through this and be in Your perfect provisions through this." As we hide under His wings, we are saying, "God, I can't do this, but You can." The whole idea is to get God's perfect direction and will for our lives. Sometimes I feel like God takes pleasure in watching us crying out, waking up at night, saying, "Oh, God, please send help," when all the time He is providing, He is moving. He hears us and helps us.

The point is that this is all for His plan. What plan? For us right now, He is saying get out of debt. We are not in a lot of debt, but it is the craziest thing that we cannot pay it off right now. I know He is able to provide for this debt. We keep asking, seeking, and knocking for God's perfect time of deliverance. I hear the Lord's direction for getting out of debt and making plans for our future in serving on the mission field.

I feel like, *Lord, why couldn't I plan for missions years ago? I feel like I have wasted so much time.* My husband feels the same way. "Oh, God, please hide us from discouragement." I must confess I haven't felt this kind of discouragement in a long time. In fact, the last time I felt this discouraged was right before I had a major breakthrough in my life. So at this point, I am looking for a breakthrough.

Speaking of hiding under His wings, in his book, *God's Smuggler*, Brother Andrew prayed as he smuggled Bibles into Russia. He was at the border of Yugoslavia and prayed, "Lord, in my luggage I have scripture that I want to take to your children across this border. When you were on earth, you made blind eyes to see, now I pray you make seeing eyes blind so that they do not see those things you do not want them to see." Hiding under the shadow on the mission field is powerful. The Holy Spirit leads us and guides us in powerful ways.

A few years ago, we went to Bolivia with one of my favorite pastors and a chiropractor. We took medical supplies so that we could hold a free medical clinic. I think we had seven duffle bags full of first-aid and hygiene items. When we arrived at the airport, we were in line, going downstairs to the check-in lines. My spirit was on alert, and as we got closer to get in line, I noticed a woman come out of one of the side doors. I watched her and noticed that she had a mean spirit. As I watched her, she headed to open up a line. I immediately tried to get the guys' attention not to go to her line, but they did. Sure enough, she grabbed all our bags and kept them. I don't even know why. We all entered the country but had no bags. Our land host was there to meet us, and he tried to intervene but with no luck.

The next day, the men said we should go and get our bags. So my husband and I stayed back and prayed while they went on. About two to three hours later, they showed up back at the hotel with all of the bags.

They decided to start at the consulate. They waited and waited, until finally realizing he was not going to see them. So one of the men decided to just go to the airport. When they got there, all the bags were right in the middle of the entrance. So they walked up to the bags. A man came out and asked, "What are these bags doing here? Who do they belong to?"

The interpreter answered, "They belong to us."

The airport guy asked, "Why are they here? What is in them?" He walked over to the bags, took the bag on top, and opened it. Inside he found men's underwear. He picked them up, threw them down, and said, "Get these out of here."

We laughed and laughed. Thank God for our friend's underwear! God delights when we hide in Him; He shows himself strong and mighty on our behalf. He'll even use underwear.

It was written that Brother Andrew's missions were fraught with peril and pathos, financed by faith, and supported by miracles. That's what I want to experience. What an amazing God we serve. He is able to keep us in every way.

The Holy Spirit speaks to us. It was He who said, "Don't go to that line. There is a mean spirit there." It is He who will say, "Go here and go there," or, "Don't turn left, turn right," or, "Go and stop." That is His voice you are hearing. Listen and act; don't be afraid.

Chapter 7

PLANT ME

That they might be called trees of righteousness, the planting of the Lord, that he might be glorified.

—Isaiah 61:3

I mentioned in an earlier chapter how Isaiah 61 changed my life. Now I expound on this chapter and various other chapters that mean so much to me. I find it amazing that Jesus read this chapter in a synagogue in His hometown of Nazareth, and the very first words that came out of His mouth were (verse 1): "The Spirit of the Lord God is upon me; because the Lord hath anointed me to preach good tidings unto the meek; the poor, the downhearted, the discouraged, the hopeless."

"The Lord has anointed me." Verse 1 gives us a look at Jesus Christ the Messiah. The word "Messiah" comes from the word *Mashiach*, which means "to anoint, to apply oil, to consecrate someone or something." Kings who were appointed to office were anointed with oil. While Old Testament kings and spiritual leaders were anointed with oil, New Testament believers are anointed with the Holy Spirit for service unto the Lord.

It is the responsibility of the body of Christ to preach good tidings. We carry the good news. Jesus said that He came not to call the righteous but sinners to repentance (Matthew 9:13). Jesus preached good tidings to those who realized they were sinners. Those who were downcast, hopeless, and poor were drawn to Jesus because He preached good tidings, good news. The same should be for us to share the gospel with those we know are not saved. It should be our prayer that those with whom we come in contact will be drawn to us because of the anointing. The Spirit of the Lord is upon you and me because the Lord has anointed us to preach good tidings to the poor.

The chapter goes on: "He sent me to bind up the brokenhearted, to proclaim liberty to the captives, and the opening of the prison to them that are bound; to proclaim the acceptable year of the Lord."

"Bind up the brokenhearted." How many brokenhearted people do you know? A lot? Some? I don't know about you, but I have had my share of being brokenhearted. It is sad to say, but there is little taught on the brokenhearted, sadness, and a broken spirit. I think women have good insights when it comes to these. I know that when God healed me through His Word, I became more sensitive to other women suffering from being brokenhearted or having a downcast spirit. It brings me joy to minister to women who have been abused or told that they are nothing. I like to see how the Lord lifts them up through encouragement by prayer and His Word.

Psalm 147:2 says, "The Lord builds up Jerusalem; He gathers together the outcasts of Israel. He heals the brokenhearted and binds up their wounds." This is so true and powerful. If God can heal the torn-up, brokenhearted person I was and make me His vessel for His use, He will use you too. He will heal you. He will save you and use you for His glory.

The Word of God healed me in so many ways. When I felt like I was such a wreck only His word brought peace and hope.

Psalm 91:2 tells us, "and the day of vengeance of our God; to comfort all that mourn." Realize that the day of vengeance of our God has to do with a judgment that will take place at the second coming. But notice that He immediately says after this to "comfort all that mourn." I find it amazing that God immediately comforts after judgment.

Psalm 91:3 says,

> *Appoint unto them that mourn in Zion to give unto them beauty for ashes, the oil of joy for mourning, the garment of praise for the spirit of heaviness (depression); that they might be called trees of righteousness, the planting of the Lord, that He might be glorified.*

I remember reading these scriptures, meditating on them, and crying out to the Lord, "God, heal me, appoint unto me beauty, take my ashes, give me the garment of praise, and heal my spirit of heaviness that I might be called a tree of righteousness a planting of the Lord that your name may be glorified." I lived on these scriptures and on Psalm 91, hiding under the shadow of the Most High God. We know that these scriptures speak of the millennium, but they also speak of our present situation.

The garment of praise for the spirit of heaviness is so important for healing the inner person. When I was in a depression, it was hard for me to praise; I felt stuck and always pressed down. I realized that it is a decision—I can either open my mouth and heart and praise Him in the midst of this, or I can decide not to put on the garment of praise. It is a decision that needs to be made every day. When your spirit begins to feel heavy, start to praise and worship the Lord. You can choose the garment of praise or the spirit of heaviness and depression. It's your choice.

Understanding Isaiah's prophecy in chapter 61 is awesome. But in my distress, the Lord met me through these verses that I now call my "life verses." I remember pressing in on worship during those tough times. Now I thank the Lord for those hard times because they helped me to realize how much He cares for people and how powerful His Word is in healing, saving, and raising people out of the depths of despair. He is able to raise one up to becoming a worshipper and lover of God.

These scriptures opened my eyes to seeing Jesus not just as my Savior, which is everything, but as the conquering King over my soul. That is the good news we need to share with those around us or those who may be living empty, broken, and hopeless lives.

Finally, verses 10 and 11 say,

> I will greatly rejoice in the Lord, my soul shall be joyful in my God; for he hath clothed me with the garments of salvation, he hath covered me with the robe of righteousness, as a bridegroom decketh himself with ornaments, and as a bride adorneth herself with her jewels.

> *For as the earth bringeth forth her bud, and as*
> *the garden causeth the things that are sown in*
> *it to spring forth; so the Lord God will cause*
> *righteousness and praise to spring forth before*
> *all the nations. This is our song, the ransomed*
> *and the redeemed believers covered with the*
> *Blood of the Lamb, robed in the righteousness*
> *of Jesus that He may be glorified.*

As I was being healed, I became more sensitive to the hurting people around me, and I wanted to help and be used by God to bring them the same kind of healing that He gave to me. The Lord began to bring women my way to disciple and encourage. He also began to use me to speak at women's groups, but He gave me an assignment that some do not use or likely accept. It involves the supernatural power of God. He started to show me what women were going through as they came up for prayer in the meetings. I would lay hands on them, and the Lord would touch them.

God wants to move supernaturally, but it appears as though the church is not open to or don't believe in the supernatural power of God. One thing I notice is that the church limits God. It is true that doubt and unbelief will stifle the moves of God. It makes me sad that the body of Christ operates in doubt and unbelief. God should be able to pour out His Holy Spirit upon us all so that we are effective for the kingdom of heaven. I think that people want to see God move, but they are, for the most part, scared of the unknown. God's power is unknown by the church because people are not being taught to expect to see God move. I have learned to wait on the Lord for His movement.

I remember as a young woman often hearing a song about the nations. I would sing along, weep, and think, *That could never be for me*. I could never be used that way. Going to the nations? That must be for some special person or people. How sad that I thought, *Oh, well, I guess I am just supposed to work to make sure that I get to heaven*. However, the real problem was that I was bored. With no challenge, no encouragement, and no vision, I had become what I saw in the church all those years. Eventually, the norm of going to church set in, and before I knew it, a sense of apathy seemed to be evident in my life.

When you're a comfortable Christian, you begin to slow down. You slow down with the passion of serving, you slow down with the compassion for the poor and lost, you slow down with worship, and you slow down on the fellowship. Yes, it's true. How many believers have I seen in this position? All too many.

I want to challenge you to attempt something big for God. For me, it's writing this book. But guess what? I want more. I choose not to settle for a one-time accomplishment. I want more—more of God, more of Christ in me, more challenges, more compassion, more worship, more fellowship, and yes, I want to serve the nations.

Psalm 2:8 tells us, "Ask of me and I will give you the heathen for your inheritance and the uttermost parts of the earth for your possession." I so want to bring the good news to the nations if the Lord will permit. Not that He needs my help, but I believe that there is a certain task only I can do. Whatever the size, I want to do it. May His name be glorified in my life and yours.

Are you ready for the challenge? Think about it for a

minute. In recent months, I had two dreams. In the first one, my husband and I were at home, looking outside. The sky was dark, and a large tornado was coming toward us. I looked closely and said to my husband, "Look, those are people. They are souls!" There were too many to count, but they were twirling and interlocked, spinning out of control. They were lost, not saved.

In the next dream, my husband and I were at the beach. We were in the parking lot, and I noticed more than the usual number of surfers on boards. The waves were getting bigger and bigger, but no one was concerned. Just then, I noticed a young guy with a panel station wagon and long blond hair talking with a few other guys. The Lord said to me, "He's the one."

I asked, "What do you mean, Lord?" He said he was the one who was supposed to go and speak the message to the ones on their boards, who were perishing. So I went to him and said, "You're the one."

"The one for what?" he asked.

I said, "You know what you are supposed to do," but he wouldn't answer me. I pointed to the others on their boards. "You're supposed to go to them." But he wouldn't look.

Listen, you and I are called to go to the ones in our fields; only the surfer can reach his friends and other surfers. The ones who are lost in the tornadoes of life are the ones we are to pray for. Pray for the lost.

I am reminded of the book of Jude. The purpose of the book is to remind the church of the need of continual vigilance, to keep strong in the faith, to encourage each other to stay in the faith, and to contend for the faith (Jude 1:3). This is a powerful verse, as Jude was expressing the need to write to the church and exhort them due to the dangers of false teaching. Well, guess what? We are to do the same. The unbelievers around us are living lives separated from God because of the false teachings of society around us. It's true.

As a final encouragement, I provide the following recap of some important spiritual insights I have shared with you:

(**A**) Jesus said, "Many are called but few are chosen." The chosen are the ones who cannot be still, the ones who are not satisfied with everyday stuff.

(**B**) If we just allow Him to be in complete control of our lives, we would be completely surprised at what He can do through us, and we would be surprised at the plan that He has for us.

(**C**) Learn His presence in your life. In my early years of salvation, I would go to see my pastor for guidance, and he would say to me, "Christine, just practice His presence. As you do this, you will begin to see and know your Savior." So I did just that. I took a few minutes to practice His presence and just love Him. That is how I learned to know His voice, worship the Word, and prayer. Always remember that the voice of God is the Word of God.

(**D**) Always run to Him and not from Him, no matter what. As we were called to go to Israel, once again I found myself crying out to the Lord for guidance, direction, and confirmation. He always meets me personally along with my path. If you ask, God will meet you along the way of your path too.

(**E**) Be a visionary. In Proverbs 29:18, a visionary relies on God's presence and revelation. The verse says, "Where there is no vision, the people perish: but he that keepeth the law, happy is he." As we train ourselves to be people of vision, the less we react to situations. I thank our Lord that as He works His life in us, we will become visionaries for His good use.

(F) Expect the supernatural for your situation or the situation of others. That is where God desires to show up. Glory to His name. Prepare for vision through prayer; vision begins in prayer, quietness, and isolation. Habakkuk was in a tower, waiting to hear from God (Habakkuk 2:1). Make sure you have a quiet place to go to be alone with God. He so longs for this time to be with you.

(G) Ask the Lord for confirmation of revelations that He gives you. Peter questioned after he had a vision of food that he refused (Acts 10:13–14). Our Lord told him specifically what was about to happen in Acts 10:15–22. The Lord will give you confirmation of your vision; be sensitive to hearing God's answer. Look for it; He will show up! Don't limit God; look for Him, and you will find Him. Look for God to do the supernatural; it is a beautiful experience.

Our status: As of today, we continue to pray and seek the Lord as to our departure date to Israel. This is the way it has been for us. We are taking care of our parents, fulfilling a vow, and getting our finances in order. Once this task is completed, we believe that we will be free to go and serve freely and without restriction. But in the meantime, we will serve where we are planted. Amen. I can hardly wait to see what God has in store!

Now as for you, my brothers and sisters, "Go" to that place that the tugging of your heart keeps longing for (Matthew 28:18).

My favorite scripture for Israel is Isaiah 43:1–5.

But now thus saith the Lord that created thee, O Jacob, and he that formed thee, O Israel, Fear not: for I have redeemed thee, I have called thee by thy name; thou art mine. When thou passest through the waters, I will be with thee; and through the rivers, they shall not overflow thee; when thou walkest through the fire, thou shalt not be burned; neither shall the flame kindle upon thee. For I am the Lord thy God, the Holy One of Israel, they Saviour: I gave Egypt for thy ransom, Ethiopia, and Seba for thee. Since thou was precious in my sight, thou hast been honorable, and I have loved thee: therefore will I give men for thee, and people for thy life. Fear not: for I am with thee: I will bring thy seed from the east, and gather thee from the west.

"Behold, he that keepeth Israel shall neither slumber nor sleep" (Psalm 121:4).

"Pray for the peace of Jerusalem: they shall prosper that love thee" (Psalm 122:6).

Printed in the United States
By Bookmasters